Praise for *The Better Life*

Practical, witty, intelligent, ;
The Better Life wooed me to
love—a simple, focused, m

—**Mary DeMuth,** author of *The Wall Around* ...

I can't say enough great things about *The Better Life*.
Each chapter had me nodding my head and having an
aha moment. Claire Diaz-Ortiz has such a wide array
of expertise. We all benefit from her wisdom with this
book. From productivity to increased happiness to
finding time for yourself, I loved the gentle reminders
and wisdom she shares. This is a book you will read again
and again.

—**Alli Worthington,** chief operating officer of Propel
Women and author of *Breaking Busy*

Sometimes we forget that the moments that allow us to
feel fully alive aren't found in what we accomplish but
who we become. In *The Better Life*, Claire reminds us
that those moments are still possible and inspires us to
make them ours, new once again.

—**Bonnie Gray,** author of *Finding Spiritual Whitespace:
Awakening Your Soul to Rest*

Claire is a force of nature—brilliant, compassionate,
unstoppable. And this book, *The Better Life*, is her
manifesto on living well.

—**John Sowers,** author of *The Heroic Path*

I read *The Better Life* in one sitting—and it made me want to be a better person. Claire's words are wise, transparent, and practical. They breathe hope into souls inundated with information and overloaded with pressure. They offer rest to the weary heart. Highly recommended.

—**EMILY T. WIERENGA,** founder of The Lulu Tree and author of six books including the memoir *Making It Home*

Claire Diaz-Ortiz is like a travel guide for life. Her stories and insights will give you a vision of where you want to go and practical steps that will help you get there. And the place you'll arrive at by the end of these pages will be more filled with joy, peace, and what truly matters to you.

—**HOLLEY GERTH,** bestselling author of *You're Already Amazing*

The Better Life is a super-motivating, practical, inspiring book that will help you live a more meaningful, intentional life without feeling overwhelmed. If you feel like you've been going through the motions and are aching to live out a better life, get this book stat!

—**SARAH MAE,** Author of *Desperate* and *Longing for Paris*

THE BETTER LIFE

small things you can do
right where you are

CLAIRE DIAZ-ORTIZ

MOODY PUBLISHERS

CHICAGO

Edited by Pam Pugh
Interior Design: Ragont Design
Cover Design: Connie Gabbert
Cover photo of gold stars copyright © by Fribus Mara / Shutterstock / 89872825. All rights reserved.
Author photo: Jose Diaz-Ortiz

Published in association with the literary agency of The Fedd Agency, Inc., Austin, Texas.

Library of Congress Cataloging-in-Publication Data

Diaz-Ortiz, Claire, 1982-
 The better life : small things you can do right where you are / Claire Diaz-Ortiz.
    pages cm
 ISBN 978-0-8024-1293-5
 1. Self-actualization (Psychology) 2. Behavior modification. 3. Conduct of life.
 4. Peace of mind. I. Title.
 BF637.S4D544 2015
 158.1--dc23

                              2014046447

We hope you enjoy this book from Moody Publishers. Our goal is to provide high-quality, thought-provoking books and products that connect truth to your real needs and challenges. For more information on other books and products written and produced from a biblical perspective, go to www.moodypublishers.com or write to:

Moody Publishers
820 N. LaSalle Boulevard
Chicago, IL 60610

1 3 5 7 9 10 8 6 4 2

Printed in the United States of America

To Lucia, who is just beginning.

CONTENTS

INTRODUCTION

This is a small book with a big message.

In these thirty-something vignettes, you'll find a host of ways to improve life as you know it, right where you are.

Every story in this short volume is a powerful, personal, prescriptive, and encouraging one. And each story offers a small way to instantly improve your current life. Sometimes I make it easy to see what you need to do to put one foot in front of the other, and sometimes it requires a bit more reflection to find the meaning at hand.

Ultimately, each story gives a calm, clear message to millennial readers of all walks of life: Take charge of your life for the better, now. No matter your circumstances, you *can* make a positive difference in your life today. *The Better Life* is a call to arms for your better life, right where you are.

I know that where you are may not be where you want to be. In fact, I hope that's the case, in the same way I hope that I will get better and bolder and brighter with each passing day in this orbit.

Each of the vignettes in this book will get you one step closer to that better life you're dreaming of. Read, take action, and transform. It's a happy road, and we're on it together.

SET YOUR INTENTIONS

L ike most of us, I want to be happier. Whether it's waking up with more spark or going to bed more satisfied with my day, I want to open my life to the opportunity for greater joy.

As such, I love to read books about happiness. My writer pal Gretchen Rubin has written a few of those, and in one of them she recommends a small, powerful idea that has taken hold to become a big, strong force in my own life.

That idea is to choose a word each and every year that represents the year you have in front of you. Rather, to choose a word *for* your year. (Oh, and take a cue from Gretchen: years don't need to start in January.) Choose one single word that imbues the type of year you wish to have, one word that can serve as a guidepost for what you want in the season to come. A singular word you can always harken back to in moments of darkness and doubt. One word that informs your decisions, crystalizes your passions and priorities, and embodies you—the new you!—in the months ahead.

Depending on the type of year you seek, there are many words that can do the trick. Words like Move, Pause, Breathe, Dance, Less, Family, Health, Travel, and Choose all hold a certain special sauce.

The guidelines are simple. The word can be a verb or a noun. It can be a long word or a short word. But it is key that the word brings together everything you fervently hope to live and breathe in the year to come. One word to inform and synthesize the year you have ahead of you. One word to mean everything you want the year to be, and one word that will help serve as a guiding light when times get tough and you're not clear on where your priorities are.

A few years ago, my word of the year was Rest.

It was a word that meant the world to me in that season of my life. I was harried and overwhelmed from a few too many years of corporate globetrotting, and I needed a daily reminder to do less. And so I did. Although my Rest might not have been as restful as the Rest that some might be able to enjoy (I saw nary a beach that entire year), my word still served as a key force in getting me to slow down. It helped me to make decisions, and to keep in mind what was really important when difficult choices arose.

Should I go to that social event—or stay home? Should I say yes to what could be a great opportunity, or pass it up to wait for something better to come along? Should I travel to that work meeting—or call into it instead?

When life and work calls for us to be busy, it is hard to slow down. However, by attempting to make this word forefront in my mind, I sought to make small strides that would lead to notable changes and positive transformation. I knew I wouldn't be perfect. I knew I would never get it 100 percent. But I did know that by setting the intention, I could make some progress.

In the end, I did. And you can, too. Set a word now, and watch your year rise up to take shape around it.

BECOME A
MORNING PERSON

I f you've heard it once, you've heard it a thousand times: The early bird gets the worm.

It turns out that cultures all over the world have concepts that convey the same idea.

Morning people get more done. Morning people are more effective. Morning people win more often.

The reality is that morning people *do* seem to get an awful lot accomplished, and even night owls have reported that short periods of morning waking have made them feel more productive, even if they really aren't.

As a self-professed night owl (or "late chronotype") who has worked hard to get up earlier, I can vouch that waking up in the morning earlier can make you *feel* you've done more. In contrast, doing a lot between 1:00 and 4:00 a.m., like many a raging night owl, invariably makes me feel behind when I drag myself out of bed at noon the next day. Waking at 5:30 a.m., watching the sunrise, and literally feeling that you beat everyone at the first competition of the day—getting up—is something that just can't be matched.

There are many reasons to try your hand at getting up earlier. Here are my favorites:

You get the best of you. If you're generally sleeping enough and you aren't suffering from health problems, then you should feel rested in the morning. In those first precious hours, you'll have energy in abundance to do what you need to do. This is the golden hour of productivity, and by getting up early you can use it to the best of your ability to kill your to-do list and really get rocking.

You get the best of others. I once heard someone say that people are nicer in the mornings because they haven't yet had the chance to have a bad day. It just might be true, and you just might benefit as a result.

You get quiet. Fewer people are around in the morning —in your house, in your office, and in the world at large. That means quiet, peaceful time for you to do what you need to do. Make the best of these moments.

Getting things done early makes you happier all day long. The earlier you get done the necessities, the better you'll feel the rest of the day, no matter what pops up to surprise you. You're also far less likely to be off-track at the end of the day, because you'll have at least gotten *something* done in the morning.

You're likely to get more done by the end of the day. Even if your workday is the exact same nine hours it might have been had you started work at eleven in the morning, by starting earlier you're likely to get time on your side through the simple art of personal motivation. The more you get done earlier, the more you're likely to get done *as the day progresses*. By the end of the day, you'll be farther along than you would have been had you started later on.

Even if you agree that waking up earlier is a good move for you, however, it's not (yet) possible to turn on a magic switch to make it happen. Instead, you've got to work a bit to make it a reality. Thankfully, it may be easier than you think. In my efforts do just this, I've learned a few key lessons:

Accept the Fact That You Will Be Tired at First

The first step in becoming a morning person is acknowledging that the initial adjustment won't be pretty. If you are not already in a state of perpetual exhaustion (I hope not!), when you try to go to bed two to three hours earlier than you normally do, it just isn't going to work. Thus, the result of the initial shift to waking earlier will be a tired, grumpy you no one wants to be around. Warn those around you, and remind yourself you're doing it for a greater cause. Better yet, try to combine it with that necessary red-eye flight you have to take, or that crying baby that just can't seem to get to sleep on her own (I have one you can borrow, if needed).

Immediately Find a Way to Reward Yourself in the Morning

Especially in the beginning, you've got to find a way to reward yourself for the effort of getting out of bed before the sun brightens the sky. What is one thing you wish you could do each day that you rarely give yourself time for? Reading a novel? Watching a TV show you love? Doing the Wednesday *New York Times* crossword (not too hard, not too easy)? In the beginning, do that one fun thing each morning to reward yourself for getting up and to make you excited to keep doing so. One day soon, you won't need it.

Start a Morning Routine

Once you've found a way to create the initial shift to getting sleepy earlier at night, and have done so for a few days in a row, you've got to find a way to develop a strong morning routine that will get you waking up at that same (early) time each morning. As we'll talk about, no one routine works for all breathing beings, and ultimately, it's all about finding a series of morning steps that work for you, and then making them automatic.

Soon enough, your (more) productive self will thank you.

TRY THE PRESENT PRINCIPLE

No matter what time you get up, having a morning routine will help ground your day. Most days, I start my mornings with a seven-step process I have come to call the Present Principle. It's a simple routine built around the simple acronym P.R.E.S.E.N.T., which reminds me to implement the seven most important things I need to do daily to keep me present—and to do those things in the mornings.

My routine won't work for everyone, but I hope it will give you the inspiration you need to come up with a morning routine of your own that will lead you to success. As you'll see as you read through mine, the key to developing a routine of your own is to identify the handful of important activities you want to accomplish each and every day, and then to front-load them into your morning.

The 7 Steps in My Morning Routine (the Present Principle):

P—PRAY (or PAUSE)

I start my days with a steaming cup of bulletproof coffee or tea and a prayer of guidance, thanks, and direction for my day ahead. Another way to think of this moment more broadly is as a "pause"—for prayer and contemplation. It's a critical way to start a busy life, day in and day out.

R—READ

After praying and pausing, I dive into reading something inspirational and motivational. I generally work through one particular devotional for a few months, and sometimes have a few going at a time. Make sure to find one that speaks to you personally, and not one that someone else loves but you think reads like fluff (been there, done that). If you aren't into the idea of inspirational or spiritual reading at this groggy hour, think about a good read on business, leadership, or productivity that you can slowly work through sections of, day in and day out.

E—EXPRESS

After reading, I then take my own thoughts to paper. I use a black Moleskine journal that has seen better days, but a Post-it note or Evernote document will do just fine. The key is just to get your feelings out there. Worries, thoughts, thanks, angst; anything and everything.

S—SCHEDULE

Now's the time in my routine that I sketch out an overview of my day and do a check-in on my week. I typically spend five minutes on this step—drafting my day's schedule and checking in on the week at large. I do this on paper, with the goal of this step being offline, but you may find it works best to use your computer or an app.

E—EXERCISE

I try to get in exercise of some sort every day (I run most days, except when my jogging stroller gets the best of me), and I find that doing it in the morning is the most effective way to keep at it. Experts say this is also smartest when working to form solid habits. Move daily, and you'll feel better.

N—NOURISH

Each day, do one thing that truly nourishes you. Go on a walk. Take a bubble bath. Read a novel. Talk to someone you love. Do something for you. It's fun to do this in the morning straightaway, but if not, put this off until later as a reward for getting your big tasks of the day done.

T—TRACK

At the day's end, look back at how many of the steps in your routine you were able to accomplish. Can you do better tomorrow? Track your progress, and think about what is working and what isn't. This will better poise you to make tweaks and win long-term.

I'm not always perfect. Some days I don't do every step, and some days I don't do any of them at all, but trying to implement this routine each and every day has been an incredible motivation for me and has given me the conviction that morning routines can make anyone's day better and brighter.

Now you try it.

SAY YES

In 2008, I was in business school in England when Biz Stone, the cofounder of Twitter, came to visit Oxford University. By that point, I had been in touch with folks on his team for a few years: first, when the original Blogger crew found and promoted my travel blog to the world; and later, when the Blogger team and Biz started Twitter and they featured me as an early user, tweeting away from my life trotting the globe and living in an orphanage in Kenya.

During my time in business school, I had been thinking a lot about what I wanted to do next with my life. I had a strange background—having spent time in both digital innovation and in the nonprofit world of social change—and I wanted to marry the two. Silicon Valley seemed like the obvious place to do so.

During Biz's visit, one of our mutual friends told him I'd take him on a tour of Oxford. I'm not a very good tour guide, though, since I get lost even in my hometown of Berkeley, where my parents have lived my entire life. So that didn't seem like such a great idea. Instead, I introduced myself after he gave a talk to my business school class, and we hung out while some reporters asked him if it was true that Facebook was trying to buy Twitter. That evening, he sent me a text, telling me to come stop by.

I go to bed early, and England is cold in October, and I was already cozy in my small turreted room at an Oxford college, and I'm one of the more introverted people you'll ever meet. I wanted to say no. I really did. But a different part of me took over. The part of me that sensed that something might happen if I went, and that I should make the effort.

And I did. I put on the big tweed coat I had bought at the thrift shop the week before and walked all the way to where he was staying, the famous old jail that is now the fancy hotel.

And that night Biz said I should come work for Twitter. (There was more to it, of course, as I talked about what I wanted to do with my career, and what he wanted to build with Twitter, and how he wanted to use the platform to change the world, and why people called him Biz anyway, but I'm skipping over that part.)

And I did.

And it was one of my best yeses.

SAY NO

The year I decided to create a word of the year was the year I also tried to learn how to better say no. It made sense, of course. My word of the year was Rest, and as I learned almost immediately, the only way to rest more was to limit the things you say yes to.

When I had a choice between X and Y, I remembered my word. When I needed to make a decision between going out or staying home, I remembered my word. When I wanted to drink another double shot espresso and fire off a string of emails to world changers about things we should do together, I *remembered my word*. And this meant I had to say no on many occasions when my normally overactive brain and body simply wanted to shout YES!

Saying NO, as everyone knows, is hard. And so I had to work to get better at it.

One day, to practice my NO muscle, I tried to come up with ninety-nine ways to best say it. Ninety-nine ways that kindly, smartly, officially ended the ask in question in favor of me having more time to say yes to something better.

My aim was that each word or phrase should be truthful, firm, and not apologetic or explanatory. Sometimes I succeeded and sometimes I failed. But I did finish that list. And this is what it looked like.

Ninety-Nine Ways to Say No

1. Not now.
2. Look! Squirrel! (This wasn't my idea, but I loved it. And I will be forever grateful to the blog reader who sent in this gem.)
3. My word of the year is Rest, so I can't fit another thing in.
4. Nope.
5. No thanks, I won't be able to make it.
6. Not this time.
7. Heck no.
8. No way, José! (Since my husband is named José, this is a favorite.)
9. Regrettably, I'm not able to.
10. It's that time of the year when I must say no.
11. It's a Wednesday. I have a "No on Wednesday" policy.

12. Ask me in a year.
13. I know someone else who might be a fit for that.
14. You're so kind to think of me, but I can't.
15. Maybe another time.
16. Sounds great, but I can't commit.
17. Rats! Would have loved to.
18. I'm slammed.
19. Perhaps next season when things clear up.
20. I'm at the end of my rope right now so I have to take a rain check.
21. If only it worked ;)
22. I'll need to bow out.
23. I'm going to have to exert my No muscle on this one.
24. I'm taking some time.
25. Thanks for thinking of me, but I can't.
26. I'm in a season of No.
27. I'm not the person for you on this one.
28. I'm learning to limit my commitments.
29. I'm not taking on new things.
30. Another time might work.
31. It doesn't sound like the right fit, but many thanks.
32. I'm resting right now.
33. I'm not sure I'm the best person for it.

34. No thank you, but it sounds lovely.
35. It sounds like you're looking for something I'm not able to give right now.
36. I believe I wouldn't fit the bill, sorry.
37. It's not a good idea for me.
38. Not now.
39. I'm trying to cut back.
40. I won't be able to help.
41. If only I had a clone!
42. I'm not able to set aside the time needed.
43. I won't be able to dedicate the time I need to it.
44. I'm head-down right now on a project, so I won't be able to.
45. I wish there were two of me!
46. I'm honored, but can't.
47. NoNoNoNoNoNo.
48. I'm booked into something else.
49. I'm not able to make it.
50. Thanks, but no thanks.
51. I'm not able to make it this week/month/year.
52. Bye now.
53. I've got too much on my plate right now.
54. I'm not taking on anything else.

55. Bandwidth is low, so I won't be able to make it work.

56. I wish I could make it work.

57. Not possible.

58. I wish I were able to.

59. If only I could!

60. I'd love to—but can't.

61. Darn! Not able to fit it in.

62. Nah.

63. No thanks, I have another commitment.

64. It's just not a good time.

65. Sadly I have something else.

66. Unfortunately not.

67. Something else will be taking up my time. Sorry.

68. Apologies, but I can't make it.

69. Thank you so much for asking. Can you keep me on your list for next year?

70. I'm flattered you considered me, but unfortunately I'll have to pass this time.

71. Unfortunately it's just not a match.

72. No, sorry, that's not really my thing.

73. Nope. Again.

74. Eeek! (no.)

75. No, I'd rather not, but thanks anyway.
76. I can't make it work.
77. It just won't fit right now.
78. I'm really buckling down on my priorities right now, so I can't.
79. No says I.
80. My family won't allow me to take this one on.
81. This isn't a good season.
82. Ick.
83. Nein.
84. Sorry, no can do.
85. I only say yes to very select opportunities, and unfortunately this doesn't meet my criteria.
86. The demands would be too much for me.
87. It's not feasible for me to take this on.
88. I wish I had all the time in the world.
89. My body double can.
90. In another life.
91. I cry, but decline.
92. My advisors won't agree to it.
93. My body says yes, but my heart says no.
94. I'm not the person you're looking for.
95. I don't have an iota of bandwidth left in my wee brain.

96. Somewhere over the rainbow.
97. If only.
98. N to the O.
99. NO.

LEARN TO REST

The year I decided to devote myself to rest was a good year.

It started badly, because I was tired and overworked and had to resort to coming up with a word to make me slow down. I had seen what happened when your body didn't rest, and it wasn't pretty.

I had seen how the hardest part about not resting is the fact that your body reacts. Because even when your mind doesn't know it needs to rest yet, your body does, and it responds in ways that are less than glamorous. You get itchy and cranky and angry at the world around you. It's not a pretty sight, and it's all because you're not taking the time you need to step out of the game so that you can get back in.

I had also seen that when you don't choose to say no, you end up having to say no, because you quite simply can't take on another thing. And I had seen that this didn't just mean saying no to the things you really didn't want to do, but saying no to the things you really did want to: Your friend's wedding. A weekend away. A dinner party with those you love. *Those* things.

When you don't rest, I learned, you just won't be able to do the things you want to.

I had seen all of this, and I knew I had to change. For just one year, I told myself, I will try to slow down. My husband was on board, and we both breathed a sigh of relief. And then the emails started coming in. Again and again people asked me to do things and go places and write things and talk to them and have more coffees with them than exist in the whole wide world. And again and again I said no. And they kept asking. And even people who knew full well that my word of the year was Rest asked just as fervently. "I know that Rest is your word of the year, but . . ." they'd begin. And it was hard to say no. But I kept trying.

And because our mind and our body are more related than we could ever imagine, the year I made Rest my word of the year was the year that one of my biggest dreams came true. After a few years of doctors and medicines and procedures, we finally heard a tiny heartbeat on a little screen that my husband says was the happiest moment of his life thus far.

And that was Lucia and she is our light and I rested to make her come true.

Do you know how to rest? You better learn, because the best things in life can come from it.

DO SOMETHING BIG

I had been at Twitter a few years when I was tasked with studying how religious leaders were using the platform, with the goal of helping them to do better. As we knew already from our research, the category of religion as a whole was rocking Twitter, getting engagement rates that dwarfed that of other verticals. Faith leaders were great at reaching their flocks with uplifting and inspiring messages on the platform.

But we wanted to do more. One of our challenges was thinking about who wasn't yet using Twitter, and working with such leaders to develop strategies to make it a powerful place for those leaders to reach the world. Pope Benedict was one such leader. If we're being honest, he was *the* leader. The main guy in the whole wide world that Twitter didn't yet have tweeting away.

When I began working with the Vatican in 2012, I had lots of doubts. I believed wholeheartedly in the power of

Twitter as an open platform for anyone to spread a powerful message, but what did that look like when you were the pope? I had been awed to work with a number of high-profile global leaders at that point, but the pope was in a different orbit. It was the pope, after all.

After many years' worth of work shoved into just as many months, it came to fruition. On a cold December morning, Pope Benedict started tweeting. My husband sat with the press photographers, and I stood by the pope's side. I wore a ponytail.

Several months later, when Pope Benedict stepped down and Pope Francis took office, the doubts began raising their ugly heads again. Would *another* pope really see the value in such a platform to reach his followers? Would all our work go to waste?

In the end, it turned out that Pope Francis was more communicative than anyone could've ever asked for, using Twitter to make powerful, provocative, even political commentary in his fervent quest to better the globe. The world called him the people's pope, and he was Twitter's pope also, a man whose smiling face could be seen in selfies the world over, and a man treasured most of all in the country of Argentina, where I live.

If someone had told me a decade ago that I'd stand next

to the pope as he sent his first tweet, I probably would have said a few things. First: What's a tweet? Then: I'm not Catholic. But life is like that, and sometimes you do things you didn't think you'd do, or you didn't even think existed.

In the end, it ended up being one of the most exciting moments of my career. It was a challenge, and a headache at times, and it gave me nights of stress and angst, and Alitalia did permanently lose one of my suitcases on one of those tiring trips, but the end result was so exciting, rewarding, and awe-inspiring that it took away a lot of those moments.

And it showed me that the big things in our lives—even the big things we cannot see—are worth working toward. One step at a time.

The big things, made up of all the small little things, really do shine.

FIND THE PEACE AROUND YOU

Most of the time, we don't see the peace around us.
Instead, we bury our heads in work and play and family
and sometimes—only *sometimes*—do we raise our heads up
out of the sand to see the calm that the world really does offer.
We may know that living in the present is key to health and
happiness, but it's hard to remember that in the midst of our
eternal days of moving parts and stressful overwhelm.

But we can try.

Every day, I work hard to remember there are a few
things I can do to try to find more peace.

Here are a few of those things:

First Thing in the Morning, Do Nothing

As I've said, I love me a good morning routine, and one
of the key steps of my morning routine is a moment of prayer

and meditation. A couple of years ago, though, I read that doing nothing—nothing at all—could also be wildly effective. So I started trying it. Nothing. And it turns out that it's one of the hardest things you could ever do. But I try. I look at the wall, I drink my tea, and I let the thoughts flow in. And I find the kind of peace and silence you achieve when doing nothing—nothing at all—is a powerful addition to a practice of prayer and meditation.

Take Mini Breaks Throughout the Day to Breathe

I once read an article in an airplane magazine that suggested you should take a mini-sabbatical. *Great idea!* I thought. *I love it!* And then it gave, as an example, the suggestion that you should put your phone on airplane mode while driving to work. And so I put down the magazine in frustration. Because if that is a mini-sabbatical then I am a ballerina. (I am not a ballerina.)

But although it's not a mini-sabbatical, it is worth doing. In general, taking mini-breaks in our daily lives is a great way to try and keep our stress and overwhelm at bay. So go ahead, pull your hands away from the keyboard, move your eyes to the horizon, and breathe. Let the thoughts come in and let the thoughts flow out. And breathe slowly all the while. I've heard it said that making sure your feet are on the floor at key moments of grounding can also help you feel more connected to what's going on around you. So try that as you breathe.

Find a Moment of Stop in Your Day

Mini breathing breaks are great, but what's even better is a ten or fifteen minute period of time where you can go full stop and do nothing, all for yourself. I find that the best way to do this—especially in a corporate environment where it's not necessarily possible to stare at the wall for fifteen minutes while others look on in wonder—is to take a short break to go on a walk. *Outside*. Combine it with a trip to get a coffee, say, or to run an errand you need to do. But in those ten minutes of walking, don't make phone calls. Don't listen to podcasts. Just walk and breathe and wait as the thoughts jamming your mind slowly rearrange themselves into calm.

These tips aren't revolutionary, and they also aren't incredibly different from one another. They follow a key theme of taking time out—in smaller and smaller doses. But they are powerful. Because they are all about finding moments to disconnect from the speeding train of your life to bring your mind and heart back to calm.

REALIZE THAT SOMETIMES IT'S NOT GOING TO BE WHAT YOU THOUGHT IT WOULD BE

After finishing my graduate degree in cultural anthropology, I once spent a summer researching the Western volunteers in an English-language teaching program that sent college students all over the globe to teach. In India, Slovakia, and Mexico, I heard the same story: volunteer teaching is hard. And in each country, I learned that the one tool that all volunteer teachers fell back on during tough times was an insane game called Hachi Pachi.

Hachi Pachi, as I learned, was a goat rodeo, where children ran and screamed and did not learn anything at all. It had to do with chairs and taking them and never having enough, and it prided itself on the fact that the moment the kids figured out the game, the game started all over again anew with the running and the huffing and puffing and the seat stealing and the mayhem. But since it was written as a potential suggestion in a footnote in a teaching manual, it was considered a classroom tool that could be used as a last resort. And boy, was it used.

One day, I was at a diner in Central Mexico talking to Mike, an exuberant college student from New York who had come to Mexico with big teaching dreams. Over the course of the summer, those dreams had been dashed. Mike confessed that he didn't think he could do it anymore.

"Teaching is just so hard," he said, hanging his head.

Lately, things had gotten to their breaking point. Mike thought he had been doing a great job. Kids from other classes had even come by his classroom to watch him teach. *They love me!* he had thought. *I am such a great teacher!*

But then, he realized, it was just the Hachi Pachi. All around the school, small kids who weren't even in his classes were muttering the improbable nonsensical phrase "Hachi Pachi" under their breath, over and over, at all hours of the day. His own students began asking for it all day, every day. Students who weren't even in his classes would sit in the windowsills of his classroom, chanting in unison for him to begin the dreaded game.

He tried to be strong.

"I will not play Hachi Pachi today," he would tell himself. "Hachi Pachi is a bad, bad thing."

Sometimes, he'd try other things. He'd play Head and Shoulders, Knees and Toes, for example, to help the kids learn English. It would work for a few minutes until no one could think of any more body parts (they didn't know much English, after all) and the children would resort to violently putting the left eye of the kid next to them into the circle, and then Mike would have to stop the game. A few times, he brought Monopoly money into class and tried to teach the kids math in an elaborate candy store idea. The kids robbed him of the money, though, and all piled on top of each other, grabbing the candy from the smaller, weaker children, leaving everyone in tears.

Without anything to structure the time, it was worse. One day, little Pedro came into class with a strange bundle in his arms. Mike thought it was a bag of cookies. It was an iguana.

"Why did you bring an iguana to school?" Mike asked. And then, shortly thereafter, "Why are you throwing the iguana?"

When Pedro wouldn't stop bashing the poor reptile into

the walls around him, Mike sent him on a timeout outside. With the iguana. When it was over, Pedro returned with a baby bird.

"You cannot bring baby birds into class!" Mike ordered.

"Just the iguana?" Pedro asked.

Mike tried, he said. He really did. He had ideals, as most new teachers do. But in the end, the only thing that gave some semblance of order to his life teaching English was that dreaded game. This was not how he envisioned his classroom, or his summer in Mexico, or his first experience teaching the next generation. He never wanted to be remembered by his students as the purveyor of that stupid game. This was, in short, not how he thought it would be.

In the end, though, he could only do so much. Throughout that summer, I watched many volunteers like Mike, who came in with lofty visions of how they could teach students a foreign language, and left knowing that, on most days, the best you could do was use Hachi Pachi to get through the day and keep the smiles on the kids' faces. And, when they hung their heads in shame, or sighed about what educational failures they had been, I smiled. And I tried to cheer them up.

Because sometimes, in every life, the best you can do is a little Hachi Pachi. And sometimes, Hachi Pachi is enough.

LIVE THROUGH
THE HURT

Many summers ago, I went on a packaged tour of China with my mother and my best friend, Courtney.

Courtney is not my sister, though I sometimes like to call her that. Instead, she is the daughter of Ann, a petite fiery woman from Mexico City, and Jeff, a mild-mannered Californian. Ann met my mother during their freshman year of college, and they became fast friends. Growing up, we spent summers backpacking with Courtney's family, and winters skiing with them.

When Courtney and I were in our teens, Ann, Jeff, and Courtney's sister died in a car accident when a man returning from a long day of fishing fell asleep at the wheel of his RV and plowed into the family Volvo. Courtney, coming back in the team van from the track meet her family had been cheering her on at, passed the accident on the highway, having no idea her family was in the car. She had a conversation with the other runners in the van about what you would do if your family were inside those cars.

Her family never showed up at Sizzler, where the team and their families were meeting for a celebratory dinner. When Courtney got dropped off at her house that night, the police were at the door.

Courtney doesn't think about her pain on a daily basis anymore. If you ask her today how the accident shaped her, she will calmly tell you what she has learned in the twenty years since that November day. She will tell you how her life changed as a result of what happened, and the ways she knows that she became a different version of who she was going to be.

Since we became adults, Courtney and I have traveled far and wide together. That summer in China was no different.

What was different on that trip, though, was that it seemed we were surrounded by pain. Everyone had a particularly terrible story to tell, and was ready and willing to share it over the hotel dumplings at breakfast.

One woman from the Midwest, after losing her first husband, had lost two teenage children in separate car accidents. Now she was married to a man who had just survived a brain aneurism. He sat there smiling on the tour bus, a visible scar on his shaved forehead. She had short spiky hair and talked fast, and we spoke at length. Not about the pain or the bad things that had happened, but about her press-on nails. She had a system for making them look great without spending a lot of money (use regular super glue, not the fake super glue they give you free in the press-on nail kits).

Several other women on the trip were in the aftermath of painful divorces, where husbands with wandering eyes had left them for younger women. One woman couldn't stop waxing on about the benefits of the online university she had gotten her MBA from. Anyone can go! And then there was Courtney, a family dead because a fisherman fell asleep at the wheel, now buying two-dollar knockoff Chanel bags on every Beijing street corner. "Does it look real?" she'd ask.

That summer in China, I was sad. I had broken up with a boy, and didn't like it, and felt upset with the world. And I went traveling to feel better, as I've done before and will do again. And these people, apparently, had done the same.

Throughout this tour, as I watched them live their lives and do their things, I wondered what it was about pain that drew people to travel. What it was about being in another land that served as a balm to hurt. What it was that made them not feel it every day.

And, of course, I drew inspiration. Because what was a silly boy in the face of what they had faced? It was just another hurt. A small hurt on a long road.

KEEP UP
THE SEARCH

I was twenty-one, or thereabouts, and in Austria. For days, I walked around the city of Vienna with a few friends in tow. We walked and walked, doing touristy things like entering museums and buying schnitzel. But most importantly, we saw the signs. Everywhere, it seemed, the city was encouraging us to go to Einbahn.

It became a sort of routine, seeing the signs to Einbahn. Walk down one street. Look at Austrian people. Stand on a corner pointing at the guidebook and debating which street to walk down. See another blue and white sign pointing to Einbahn.

Again and again we asked ourselves the same questions: Where is this Einbahn? How do we get there, and what will we find once we arrive? And why isn't Einbahn in the book? (There was no Einbahn in the guidebook to Vienna.)

Einbahn, for us, became the elusive, perfect tourist destination—the intellectually stimulating site where we would feel at one with a different culture. We were confident that, if found, the bliss of Einbahn would reward its seeker many times over for the challenging journey. It would give everyone seeking her place in a new world the feeling of home.

Now, if you have never been to Einbahn, I don't want to spoil things for you. Because far be it for me to ruin your quest. But let's just say that it isn't exactly what we thought it was: the perfect destination and all. Let's just say that one could travel the world endlessly and never quite find Einbahn.

Our quest, in all true senses of the word, was a failure. We never found Einbahn, because, of course, it wasn't there to be found. But the other things we found along the way made it worth the journey. We saw beautiful churches and went to an opera and were moved by a small Holocaust museum and ate Sacher torte and learned all about why Wiener schnitzel doesn't mean hot dog at all. In the end, it was all well worth the days we spent searching for something that never existed.

I imagine it's like that with a lot of things we do in life. We look, not knowing what we're looking for, or where it is, and sometimes we find it. And sometimes we don't. But it was the looking that was important.

Einbahn, for locals, means one-way street.

BE OPEN TO SEE

I never meant to live in Kenya.

In 2006, I spent a year traveling the world with my best friend, Lara. It was a year of pleasure, a year of excess, and a year devoted to living for me. I went skydiving in South Africa because I felt like it, and ran through swirling Indian monsoons, laughing the whole way. I spent entire days on empty beaches, reading hundreds of books, just because I could.

I lived for me.

At the end of that trip, I arrived in Kenya to climb a mountain. I was a runner, a hiker, someone who had run marathons and climbed to Everest Base Camp and wanted more. I longed for another challenge.

When an acquaintance suggested a guesthouse near the base of the mountain where we could stay the night before starting my trek, we agreed at once. It was cheap, after all, and as broke travelers living off my freelance work, that was all we needed. When I heard the guesthouse happened to be on the grounds of a Christian orphanage where 170 little souls lived out their lives, it meant nothing to me.

It was just a place to lay my head.

The day we set out to travel to the guesthouse, a van pulled up at the gate of our hostel in Kenya's capital of Nairobi. In a hint of all the over-the-top hospitality that was to come, I had been told that the orphanage had arranged for their only car to make the eight-hour round trip to pick us up.

When it pulled up, "Imani Children's Home," emblazoned across its side, I saw a dozen teens crammed in the back.

"Are they all orphans?" I whispered to Lara.

I had never met an orphan before.

That afternoon, after a long and dusty drive with the teens, we arrived at a small campus of bright green gardens and white and blue buildings—a church, an orphanage, and a guesthouse stood proudly in the sun.

"Imani," it said everywhere.

It means *hope*, said one of the teens.

Tumbling out of the van, I breathed it all in, feeling a stirring of a sort I hadn't known. When the elders of the orphanage invited us to lunch, we readily agreed.

It was in the middle of that lunch that something changed for me. Asking to use the restroom, I found myself in a clean room off the side of the church where a mirror hung over a spotless sink.

And it was in that moment that God spoke to me. With a feeling I had never had before and have never had since, I became convinced He was with me, and I delivered my plea.

If You have put this place in the road to change me, open my eyes so I can see.

Within hours I was thinking about staying longer at this strange place. Within hours I had met the boy I would later welcome into my family, bringing him to a new life in the United States, and changing both of our lives forever. Within hours, I told Lara I would not be climbing the mountain with her.

(I never have climbed that mountain.)

A week later, I left Africa to spend a happy holiday with my family before returning to Kenya, where I lived out the year in an apartment on the ground floor of that orphanage, starting a small nonprofit organization called Hope Runs.

Every day, I huffed and puffed alongside lanky Kenyan teens and tiny girls in party dresses, holding my hand all the way, as we'd run to the next bend.

The year in Kenya forever changed me, giving me a story I never thought I would live.

All because I had been open to see.

BE WHO YOU ARE

I am not a runner.

Throughout my early life, I ran because someone else told me to. My father, say, when I was particularly grumpy. Or a coach, maybe, in the early dawn hours of a high school sports practice. In college, I joined a generation of women who listened to the advice in women's magazines that said running was good for us. I ran. I never liked it, but I kept it up. I gave my word I would never run a marathon.

In my midtwenties, when traveling around the world, I went back on this declaration. My first marathon, in Madrid, hooked me, and I went on to do three others—two in the same week, once—and another while training a bunch of Kenyan teenagers at the orphanage.

I don't run as long anymore, and I'm not nearly as dedicated.

When my daughter was a month old, and I laced up my running shoes for the first time since her birth, I realized

I hadn't run in nine months. A record for me, I thought strangely, realizing how long I had been running so regularly. I was worried about starting again after so long.

In this new beginning, I told myself I would run eleven minutes, and eleven minutes I did.

Within a week, this number was fourteen, then fifteen, until it crept up to twenty-one, where it has handily stayed for more than six months. (The running stroller has gotten dramatically heavier, I reason.)

Throughout it all, though, you'd be hard-pressed to find me saying I'm a runner. My husband might say it. My mother, perhaps. A friend. But me?

No, I'd say. I'm so *slow*, I'd say. I only run *twenty-one minutes*, I'd say.

But I'm wrong, of course, because we are the things we do. I run nearly every day and I buy running pants in bulk and when I wake up late and we have to be somewhere my husband knows I'll plead, "Can I just go on a run first *real quick*?"

And so I look back, and I see that I am the runner I say I'm not.

I am a runner, because I am who I am.

And you are who you are, deep down and underneath all that you say you aren't. Be who you are, and not who you think you cannot be.

CELEBRATE
YOUR REAL LIFE

The day before my mother hosted a baby shower for me, she and I went to a nice one for a dear friend.

A *really* nice one. At a beautiful house where there was catered Mexican food and cute Mexican decorations and an adorable little bar set up for folks to pour sweet Mexican drinks into.

We played simple games—guess how many creepy plastic babies are in this floral arrangement, guess how many jelly beans are in the jar, guess the date the baby will come —and got thoughtful prizes when we won. (I didn't win.)

There was a lovely art station where every letter of the alphabet was beautifully written with calligraphy and we all drew in an object for that letter so that the baby could have a personalized alphabet book one day. (I got *F*; I drew a falafel.)

And nicest of all, it wasn't over the top. Instead, it was beautifully casual. Perfectly lovely in the simplest of ways. In life, after all, there isn't much better than a wonderful afternoon with good friends and great guacamole.

But as my mother and I were driving away after the shower ended, I could tell she wasn't in perfect spirits.

"We're not really having *that* kind of baby shower," she finally said, nervously, laying out her apprehension.

And I knew what she meant. Because her house is smaller, and my father's backyard tomato plants have never made the garden look very orderly, and I've never planned an event in my life. (No, really, ask my husband.)

This was my baby shower:

We planned it a week before, when I told my mother I actually had decided I wanted one. I sent evites, which several friends said they never received. We got lasagna at Costco and borrowed chairs from neighbors. We put a sign up in front of the doors to my parents' back deck—"No Trespassing"—because the rotted-out deck could likely break an ankle or two. We did the game where people could guess the date of the baby's birth, and my mother found an old Dave Ramsey Financial Peace board game to give away as the prize. She would ship it to the winner, she said.

And, for all those reasons (not just the Dave Ramsey

Financial Peace board game), it was not a baby shower you would see on Pinterest.

But did I care? Not really.

Because, of course, it wasn't about that. Instead, it was about the people, as all baby showers are, really. Many of them my mother's friends, some of them mine, and two of them people who had, long ago, attended the original baby shower. The one thirty-two years before, when my mom was getting ready to welcome me into the world. A baby shower that, all in all, was probably pretty much the same—save for the deck being new that time around.

DO A GOOD
THING FOR YOU

Every time I listen to music I like while I work, I think of my old colleague and friend Maggie.

Maggie was already at Twitter when I started in 2009, moving and shaking and generally doing cool stuff. One day, at some point during the years we worked together, she sent an email to employees sharing a simple, special experience she had had that day.

Here's what happened to her:

In the middle of an otherwise busy workday, she plugged in her earphones and *listened to music*.

That was it. She listened to music. Music she liked. Music she could rock out to. Music that wasn't just white noise or classical or sounds to make the background chatter go away. Music that made her dance ever so slightly in her chair.

And it was this small experience that she wanted to

share with the rest of her colleagues.

What could we do today to make life and work a little better right where we are? Maggie asked us.

Could we turn on music? The Killers? Or what about Modest Mouse? And then could we turn up the volume a little higher?

Or was there something entirely different we could do? Something that had nothing to do with music at all and everything to do with us being just a little bit happier? Could we take a break and get a latte down the street? Could we walk to Whole Foods and buy a small bunch of flowers for our desk? Could we spend five minutes laughing with a colleague?

The question was simple, powerful, and important: What could we do today to make our life—right where we are—just a little bit better?

It's been a number of years since she sent that email. A short little email with a big and powerful message. And yet I still remember it often. Daily, if I'm good.

What one good thing could you do today?

LEARN TO WASTE TIME WELL

'm not always good at wasting time.

When I don't try, I can be found on some Saturday mornings lying on a couch watching a soul-sucking reality television program as a few too many hours tick by. Although this works on occasion to give me a break, it's not a way to provide consistent *rejuvenating* relaxation. And it's not something I would ever recommend to others. (Unless you, also, believe in the power of *Top Chef* to heal your soul.)

There's a whole other kind of relaxation that I would recommend to others, though, and I like to call it *rejuvenating* time wasting. Or rather, wasting time well.

When I'm on my game, and remembering my larger goals for my year and my life, this is how I try to spend my leisure time.

It was a book by Laura Vanderkam that first opened my

eyes to this concept. As she says in *What the Most Successful People Do on the Weekend*, if you want to waste time well, you need to plan it.

Don't outline every moment of the time you plan to waste, but rather create an overall arch for the leisure activities you aim to get done. She calls them "anchor events," and she suggests that an average weekend should have a few (three to five, say) that your days off can be built around.

Here are a few examples of anchor events that would work to build a weekend around:

Visit the flea market on Sunday afternoon.
Have a family barbeque on Saturday night.
Go to that new brunch spot on Saturday morning.
Finish the novel you're reading on Friday night.

None of these are over the top or huge, but all of them are distinct ideas with a specific time frame in mind.

By coming up with anchor activities, and setting an estimated time frame to accomplish each one, you'll allow yourself to feel you've had a productively relaxing weekend—and you'll have a great time doing it. After all, if you pick a few activities you know you will like, you're bound to enjoy them. (There's a reason you're not picking activities like "work on book proposal" and slotting them into Saturday morning as a way to relax.)

The key to wasting time well—whether on a weekend, a day off, or an afternoon—is not to over-schedule or be overly ambitious in the selection of your anchor activities. You should not put "Go to Egypt" on your list, for example. You should especially not put "Go to Egypt" followed by "Potty Train Your Toddler" on your list. Be reasonable about what you (and your child) can accomplish. It's also important to remember that we all need varying degrees of activity. For some, the act of going out too many times (whether on a bike ride or out to brunch) might not be relaxing at all. In which case your anchor events should err on the side of "bake a cake" or "plant the roses" or even "watch *Top Chef*."

(I had to sneak that in.)

Try this strategy, and discover as you come away that you're not only relaxed and refreshed, but rejuvenated at the end of a weekend off the clock.

QUIT SOMETHING
EVERY WEEK

My friend Bob Goff is a crazy man.

He is one of the most accomplished people I have ever met. He runs a law firm and a nonprofit organization (yes, both), serves as the Honorary Consul to the Republic of Uganda (yes, really), and is a *New York Times* bestselling author. But the best part about Bob? He seems to *enjoy life* more than most. Stress? Anxiety? Worry? I'm sure he has all three, but it's certainly hard to see. He is *happy*. And kind. And comes up with wild capers that he involves others in that change hearts and lives on a daily basis. Plus, he took me on my first seaplane.

Meeting Bob changed my life, and I know I'm not the only one. Because he's that kind of guy.

There are many reasons for Bob's incredible success in life, but one of the reasons I like most is his passion for a particularly strange habit: quitting one thing every Thursday. He calls it **Quit Thursday**, and it's as easy as it sounds. Every Thursday, Bob quits one thing. And every Thursday, Bob tells those around him to think about doing the same.

The idea, of course, is that we're all doing things we don't need to be doing. Things that zap our energy and passion and crowd our lives so much that we can't do the amazing things we *should* be putting all our passions into.

There's a problem with this life, and it has to do with having so many shiny choices around us that it's easy to fill up our lives with things that aren't essential. Things that don't move us toward our goals, things that don't lead our families to love, and things that don't carry our hearts to happiness. There are always more books to read, and dinner parties to host, and TED talks to watch, and small groups to start, and playdates to set up. And every day, we add more of these things to our already overflowing lives. But as our plates get fuller, we lose track of where we're going and what is really important. That's the idea behind Quit Thursday.

The concept is that every week you choose one thing you can stop doing, one thing that by stopping will bring you closer to who you really are and what you are really meant to be doing. It can be a big thing or a small thing. An easy thing to quit, or a very hard thing to let go of.

Go ahead, try it. What is one thing you can throw out of your life for good that will help you be happier, more focused, more fulfilled, and better able to accomplish what your real calling in life is? Because that's the thing you need to quit today.

Sometimes it can be hard to think of things you need to quit. Remember to go with your gut, and try not to overthink or second-guess yourself. Often—when it comes to Quit Thursdays and life in general—your first instinct is your best instinct.

STOP BEATING YOURSELF UP

When I first began to talk about Bob Goff and Quit Thursdays on my blog, something strange started happening. Again and again, I started to hear from folks who said the number one thing they wanted to quit doing was to quit beating themselves up. So, instead of folks saying they wanted to quit *doing* a particular thing, I heard that folks wanted to quit *beating themselves up* for doing that particular thing

The list of things people beat themselves up for is nearly endless. Because, it turns out, we're really hard on ourselves. At any moment of any day, many of us can be found beating ourselves up for a host of things.

For biting our nails.
For waking up late.

THE BETTER LIFE

For getting upset with a screaming five-month-old.

For wishing we hadn't bought that dog.

For watching *Top Chef* for three hours.

For being happy that our kids are grown and out of the house.

For being happy when we don't have to babysit our (wonderful) grandchild every day of the week.

For being happy when our boss is out of town (and the pressure is off).

For not having as many children as we'd like.

For not wanting more children.

For screaming at our husband that one time.

For being rude to the customer service representative.

For not standing up to the customer service representative.

For not standing up for ourselves in general.

For being annoyed at our mother-in-law.

For being annoyed at our sister.

For being annoyed at our children.

For being annoyed at our husbands.

For not reading as much as we'd like.

For not sleeping as much as we'd like.

For not exercising as much as we'd like.

For not eating as well as we'd like.

For generally not being half as awesome a person as
we'd like to be.

For generally not doing absolutely every little thing and
taking on every opportunity that ever comes our
way.

For not working enough.

For not spending enough time at home.

For, well, everything.

We can all acknowledge that there are things we all do that we'd be better off getting rid of—things that take up space in our lives that aren't helping us be our best selves. One of those things, though, is the way we make ourselves feel bad about the not-great choices we make. I'm all for making better decisions and living better lives. But there is motivation, and there is self-flagellation. I'm in favor of the former.

Quit Thursday is perfectly primed to help you stop beating yourself up. And if Bob were here, he would tell you: Whatever it is you are beating yourself up for, quit it. Put down the guilt and step away from the problem.

Do it on Quit Thursday, or on any day of the week.

What can you quit beating yourself up about?

REMEMBER PRACTICE MAKES PERFECT

A few years ago, a woman I know had a baby. It was a natural birth. It was also a home birth. It was also her fifth.

A mere hour or so before giving birth, she was apparently chatting on Skype with some other friends, saying it was time to put on some mascara (for the post-birth baby photos) before going ahead and pushing out the baby. Shortly thereafter, she did just that, and welcomed her sweet fifth babe into the world.

Although I tend to think she is a superhuman and no worldly rules apply to her, there is another theory.

It goes something like this: My friend had practiced giving birth so many times (through birthing four children previously) that she had perfected the art of what she was doing (giving birth).

Malcolm Gladwell is known for saying that 10,000 hours of practice in any field can lead to mastery. Although birthing five children may or may not add up to 10,000 hours (it depends on how you count), I still believe that mastery in this case was achieved through practice.

Birthing five children is, after all, more practice than the average American woman gets, so there is a reason that my friend is much better at birthing than I was when I gave birth to my first child. (For reference, the highlights of my birth story involved breaking down on the side of the road and having to take a taxi to the hospital, convincing my husband that eating an enormous spicy chicken quesadilla was a good idea, and live-tweeting the entire thing.)

However, I also believe that practice—whether in terms of 10,000 hours or five precious infants—is gained not simply through putting in the time. There are three key elements to practice that must be present in order to achieve perfection.

And working these three elements into the task at hand is key.

1. Do it many times. Whether it's planting an herb garden, delivering a speech, or trying your hand at Sudoku, you must do the act many, many times. There are no shortcuts to escaping the most obvious—and most necessary—aspect of practicing to reach perfection. Do the work.

2. Do it in different ways. If I want to master the art of roasting a chicken, I can't simply slice a garlic clove in half and shove it up every bird. (Nor can I listen to multiple audiobooks about Julia Child on my morning runs and hope that that does the trick. Believe me, I've tried.) Instead, I need to change my approach in order to find the best way to achieve a perfect roast. Lemon, pepper, rosemary, and other seasonings and techniques are important things for me to try. Watching reality television while doing so, or attending to the needs of a whiny six-month-old, or having an argument with a customer service representative from Verizon, might also be elements to throw in. Some might work. (Some might not.)

3. Track what works (and what doesn't) to get better with each and every try. Without measuring your success (or lack thereof), you don't know what is working. When I first started blogging in 2006, my strategy for traffic generation mirrored the way my father makes rice. Sometimes he boils the water and then adds in the rice. Sometimes he puts the rice into the water cold and then turns on the fire. Sometimes he brings the water to a boil and then turns off the heat to let the rice cook. Like my initial blogging strategy, he has no rhyme or reason, and no reliable measure by which he determines what works best. (I have told him to fix this. He does not listen.) Unlike my father, over time I started actually keeping note of what I was doing when blogging to determine what was working. *This* is what helped me get better. It's the same thing with the chicken, or the garden, or the Sudoku. (It is, according to my father, not the same with the rice.)

Ultimately, practice is not just about the time you put in, but the *type* of hours you dedicate to the task at hand. Set aside the time. And make sure it's the right time. Then watch yourself win.

GIVE THANKS

I met Ann Voskamp on the Interwebs. And when I read her bestselling book, a startlingly beautiful look into the grace of thanks, I was speechless. Speechless at the power of *One Thousand Gifts*—a book of words so well woven that it couldn't help but speak to my heart from the very first page. Speechless at her sweet life—a farm, six kids, a husband who works the land. And speechless at her big idea—that thanking God for the things we have and see and hold each and every day is the key to it all.

And so, inspired by Ann, I began a long journey of trying to give more thanks. She wasn't the first person who had ever told me to keep a gratitude journal, or to give thanks each day, or to start my morning prayers with a note of thanks. But her words affected me in a way that others had not, and it was with her inspiration that I began putting one foot in front of the other, trying to give thanks more regularly than I ever had before.

I have learned things along the way.

I have learned that taking things for granted is the easiest thing to do. We know this of course, and we hear it again and again, and some of us have it beaten into our brains from church sermons, or inspirational books we buy in airports, or wise friends. But we still cannot remember it, and every time we step off a peak into one of life's lesser valleys, we find ourselves missing the good times, and realizing that we never knew how easy we had it, and how lacking in gratitude we really were.

I have learned that the best things in my life are the things I am most likely to take for granted. It is the big things—a loving husband, a healthy baby girl, a roof in the winter—that are the easiest to never remember. And even when I make myself name them each day—José, Lucia, our home—I realize the last thing I am doing is doing them justice. Because the repetitive wonder of it all—whether in my life or in my journal—blinds me to the joy.

And so our challenge is to find a way to not shield ourselves from the joy and the grace of our very best things. And this is hard, and I do not know the way.

And so every day, I try. I try to give thanks in the things I know I can do.

I can smile wide. I can spot a bird. I can blink my eyes.

I can take a sip of water. I can sign my name. I can bite into a cupcake. I can wave to a friend. I can look at the sun. I can breathe in deep. I can spot a star. I can turn a page. I can pick up a baby. I can catch a snowflake. I can clip a flower. I can blow a kiss. I can hug a friend. I can lick an ice cream cone. And I can give thanks along the way.

These are the things I can do to thank God for this life.

LIVE THE LIFE
YOU CHOOSE

One of my favorite books of all time is a memoir about the experience of Jamie Zeppa, a Canadian woman who moves to the country of Bhutan to teach English. At one point in *Beyond the Sky and the Earth*, after the author has been in Bhutan for a while, she decides she must break up with her boyfriend back home. Her life has grown too large for him, she realizes, and he no longer fits. I have felt this in my own life at times, and know it is something we must always stay vigilant for: The people you are with need to be fit for your journey.

Years ago, shortly before one of my best friends got married, she wrote me a long letter. She is a woman with many dreams, and in the months leading up to her wedding she worried about the fact that getting married meant choosing one dream over another: the Peace Corps or the minivan.

Will I never have an exciting life if I settle down? she worried, as she shopped for white dresses and loved her fiancé fiercely.

At the time, I was far from marriage and was traveling the world. I was the one in Kathmandu, and she was the one working a steady job and buying a condo back at home. And likely we each felt moments of jealousy and envy for the other—the other option, the one not on the table.

When I read her letter, it made me think about how the lives we end up in are really just one version of the lives we could lead. In the same way that this friend of mine has never believed in soul mates—there are many different people you could live a good life with, she says, and I agree—it is the same with the lives we lead.

The night after I read her letter, I had a dream in which it went the other way—she leaves her fiancé, she moves to Botswana, and years later she says it is the best thing she ever did. But when I woke I knew that the dream didn't mean that was the path she should take because I truly didn't think it was. She had met a wonderful man and they would live a wonderful, exciting life together, even if the Peace Corps wasn't a part of that excitement. Instead, the dream just meant that we are all adaptable, and that we can live many great lives. The one with the picket fence, and the one in the

African bush. And that both lives—for this friend—and for others, can be the right choice.

And so the next morning, I wrote her back what I knew to be true: that everyone has doubts, and without them it would mean we are not realizing the magnitude of the choice we are making. And that we will always be giving up one thing for another in our quest to live our one life.

As Jamie Zeppa says, anyone can live anywhere.

Figure out where you will live, and live it well.

DO GOOD

The first summer I spent in India, I was researching volunteer English teachers who were working in a nonprofit organization. The second summer, I was also watching someone else do good. This time it was in the middle of my trip around the world with Lara. She hadn't yet gone to medical school, and she wanted to spend some time in India volunteering and taking medical classes to confirm once and for all that this was the path she should take.

That summer, we talked a lot about doing good. Mostly because I wasn't doing any of it to speak of. Instead, I was lying around Mumbai reading books, or traveling south to go to beaches, or going on dates with a Bollywood actor I had met. If you had held a gun to my head, I could not have told you what I planned to do with my life. It was around this time that my friend Amalia, a writer, had an existential crisis back in California. "Can I still be doing good if I'm a writer?" she wrote. "Maybe I should be doing something like politics.

At least writing about politics could be good, right?"

We wrote about it back and forth (I had a lot of time), and in the end we decided that doing good means different things. Ultimately, no one can tell you how to be good, even when it feels that way. Because sometimes it can be good to be Mother Teresa and help orphans, and sometimes it can be better to be a food writer in San Francisco, or to be an actor in Bollywood. The key is just to come up with your own standards and definition of what doing good means to you.

Eventually, I ended up doing some good in life. I lived in an orphanage for a year. I started a nonprofit. I became the guardian to Sammy, and brought him to the United States. But most of the good I have done so far has just been in the way that I have tried to live, which was the whole thing we were trying to figure out that summer.

I once knew a seminary student who was trying to decide what to do in life. Before seminary, he and his wife had been working in the church, and the decision of whether to continue in the church after seminary, or step out of the church, was forefront in their minds. They didn't know what to do.

One night, his wife was telling me about the problems of working in the church itself, and saying she just didn't know if seminary had been the right choice, and if she and her husband really wanted to be "professional" Christians. They had considered landscape architecture, for example, and what it would be like to own their own business. "Maybe we should just be really nice to our employees and that would be how we could best serve," she said.

Because maybe that is the answer.

I know these people still, and I know what they chose to do, and I could tell you now. But I'd rather not.

Because either choice can be doing good, and that is the real point of doing well.

REMEMBER IT'S JUST STUFF

One Easter day in 2007, when I was living in the orphanage in Kenya, I put on my Easter Sunday dress. My Easter Sunday dress that year was a drab green dress from Old Navy circa 1993 that I had bought at a garage sale when I had been living in Mexico for the year after college. It was very ugly. But because I had not yet worn it, and because Lara and I had lost all sense of fashion that year, Lara told me how nice I looked.

At church that morning, all the little girls were wearing their Easter Sunday dresses. That their Easter Sunday dresses were actually the same dresses that they run in was just one more reminder of how truly few possessions most of them had.

Hence it was notable that the sermon that day was about stuff—about what riches are, and what riches aren't. Paul, a young missionary living at the orphanage, gave the sermon, and referenced some studies showing that stuff—beyond the basics for what you need for survival—doesn't make people happy. The topic of excess was a provocative one in such an environment. The children, by virtue of an upbringing deprived of most things, had both a fascination with things and an assumption that they would never have them.

After church, we began an adapted Easter egg hunt. There were no eggs in this hunt. Eggs were precious, after all, and the children got one egg a week to eat on Sundays. Instead, we hid business cards with Bible verses on them that some company had sent me for free. Although it is was hard to imagine many kids in the United States getting too excited over these, the kids at Imani were different, and I'd been holding on to these cards for just such an occasion, knowing they'd be a hit.

That day, Lara and Missionary Paul and his wife, Stephanie, and I hid the cards all around the orphanage—in the fields, in the gardens, in the dining hall. And, given that the hunt was for only small children, we could've taken care to hide many of the cards in easy to find places, like we would have done back home. However, things were different at Imani. Because we knew that these children, who have so little, can find anything anywhere. And we soon saw that any tiny child could find a business card buried somewhere under the dirt in a two-acre spread of land in under five minutes.

And that, of course, is the nature of stuff: when you have few things, you are good at recognizing that the things you have are important, and good at making sure not to lose them. But as soon as you get more things, you want even more. And so it made sense that the 150 business cards we had at the beginning of the hunt turned into 81 at the end, with many a small child hiding a bulging pocket and avoiding our gaze when we wondered aloud where the cards had disappeared to. Because that is what it was like to be an orphan without abundance.

In an episode of *Friends*, Monica and Chandler arrive at the resort where they will be spending their honeymoon only to find that the couple directly in front of them in the hotel check-in line has just been given a complementary upgrade to the honeymoon suite. When Monica and Chandler overhear this, they ask for the same upgrade. They are told that that was the only one. They become angry and bitter and begin pouting about, huffing and puffing about the injustice. Meanwhile, the lucky couple nuzzles each other's necks and says how the upgrade doesn't matter to them at all—it's their love that counts, not the stuff.

Monica, hearing this, looks at Chandler and the concierge and replies: "We need the stuff."

And stuff is like that. We think we need it, but we don't.

LEARN THE ART
OF HOSPITALITY

I f I am particularly bad at something, it likely means I have a lot of books on the topic.

I have a lot of books on hospitality.

It has never been something I was great at. When I was growing up, my house was smaller than the ones all of my friends lived in, and although people crammed in at our place more often than anywhere else, I couldn't help but feel embarrassed at times. Later on, I realized how introverted I really am and why that means I become so drained even in large groups of my most favorite people, and I tended to eschew large social events in favor of one-on-one time. Then I spent many years traveling, and when your home is temporary, it hardly feels important to make hospitality a priority. It was while living in Africa that I began to think about the importance of giving hospitality a true home in my adult life.

In Kenya, I saw hospitality again and again. One day, I showed up to lunch at a church elder's home with three extra guests. She had no power and had spent a day cooking on a charcoal stove, but smiled graciously at the thought of feeding three more. The more the merrier. Another day, the nine-year-old daughter of the orphanage's manager invited me into her apartment. Her mother was out working, but she was more than excited to play host. After telling me to sit down on the couch, she went into the kitchen, only to reappear with a bag of white bread, a large machete, and a plastic container of Crisco. She smiled wide.

Those people knew hospitality.

And so, right when I was thinking about how I needed to better understand this hidden art, I got married. And I didn't marry just anyone. I married an architect, who makes perfect homes (ours) and throws perfect weddings (ours) and makes perfect parties (ours). (I'm just being honest.)

This is how it works: I wake up on Saturday, knowing we have a dozen people coming over for lunch, as we often do. He is already working hard away, making sure that everything that was already spotless (he accepts nothing less) is even more so. The garden, the pool, the house of glass, you could already eat off all of it. The food is lovely and the table settings are lovelier. Potluck is not in his vocabulary, and he likes using the good silverware.

I ask what I can do to help, and he says nothing. After a few more asks, he finally gives me a job. A small one. A tiny one, if we're being honest. Something I surely can't screw up. And so I try my hardest to accomplish the task, likely the same one I have been given endless times before, but I still don't do it so well. He smiles, like you might at a small child, and continues finishing everything else.

When the people come, they *ooo* and *aaa*, and stay forever, as they do in Argentina at dinner parties and social events. And they thank us for all that we've done, and I say I did nothing—which is the God's honest truth—and I smile at my husband because he has learned the art of hospitality better than anyone I know. And it is because of him that I can limp along, riding his coattails and learning bit by bit along the way.

WORRY LESS

While I was living at the orphanage in Kenya, my younger brother once came for an extended stay.

On Tony's last day in Kenya, he gave a note to Jane, age nine, and her little brother, who we called the Little Dictator (because of his name, not his demeanor). Within hours, they were more depressed than we had seen them in a long time. A clarifying conversation between Tony and the Little Dictator did nothing to resolve the situation, and the Little Dictator simply stared despondently at the ground. Things only got worse upon Tony's actual departure.

The culprit, it turned out, was Tony's handwriting. In the very sweet note he had written them, in which Tony told the Little Dictator that he really was Walker Texas Ranger (the children's favorite hero, also blond, like Tony) and that the Little Dictator was Jimmy (Walker's African American sidekick), Tony had also made a gross error in the eyes of the children.

Specifically, he had written—twice no less—"I Love You NO Much." Jane and her brother were devastated, and could not be swayed from their conviction that Tony hated them.

Painstakingly, we tried again and again to show them that in American shorthand cursive it actually read—twice!—"I Love You SO Much."

When we finally turned around their understanding of the note, and saw their shy smiles return, I breathed a sigh of relief. And I thought long and hard about how many times in life we spend our time and energy and pain worrying about things that never really happened anyway and never will. I am better at this than anyone I have ever met. I can get into a tizzy just thinking about a theoretical something that has no actual bearing on my life but might, potentially, someday, touch someone I might one day meet. And so every day, I have to try. Try to remember that worrying won't get me anywhere and that most of the things I worry about will never happen or have never happened.

And it is hard, but I keep trying.

EXPECT MORE
FROM LIFE

My dear friend Lana once met a man she really liked. Things were going well, and they had gone out a few times. One day, he picked her up for dinner and as they walked to his car she almost tripped on a bird on the sidewalk. Triggered, she began to wax on about her deep hatred of the species. "Birds, in general, are rude," she told him. She talked about all the many times in her life they had let her down, and how that terrible movie had solidified it all, and how she never wanted to even be near birds, if she were being honest.

And then she opened up about the one particular bird in her past that had turned her against the whole lot of them. Her archnemesis, Panama. Her mortal enemy for a brief moment in time.

When Lana was twelve, her aunt had to move to Japan and couldn't take her green parrot along with her, and so moved him into Lana's house. He squawked, and talked too much, and annoyed everyone—most of all Lana—and she wished fervently for the day he would leave forever. When one day the family came home to find the cage door open and Panama gone, the family joke became that Lana had hated him so much that she had thrown him out.

In truth, no one knew what had happened to Panama. They looked high and low. They canvassed the neighborhood. Lana, true to her good-hearted nature, tried hard to find the bird she hated. But the bird never came home, and they always did wonder what had happened.

Her date, at this point, began telling about his own bird experiences. Quickly, he dove into the most poignant bird story of his own childhood—when one day a bird flew into the screen door of his parents' house. It was pretty and green and spoke Spanish. They tried to figure out whose parrot it was (parrots not being on every street in their San Diego neighborhood), but no one ever claimed him. So they named him—Gizmo—and raised him. To this day, he still lived with his family.

"He's a real great bird," he said.

It didn't take long for them to look at each other. And for one of them to raise an eyebrow. And for one of them to understand. Two people. Raised in the same neighborhood of

San Diego, one who had found the hated, lost bird of the other and raised him these past twenty years. They were giddy with the craziness of it all, and Lana began texting her family.

"That filthy bird?!" Lana's brother wrote back. "Panama?!"

Her date did the same.

"The original owner of Gizmo?" her date's brother wrote. And then, concerned, "Does she want him back?!"

But it can't be, they said, not willing to believe it.

And so Lana's date showed Lana a picture of the parrot today, to confirm, and Lana breathed a sigh of relief. Because, of course, although it had the exact same face that Panama did, it had a weird yellow streak. And Panama had no yellow on his face. Lana was sure of it. But he really did look the same.

Lana sent her brother the picture. "It's not him."

Minutes later, her brother called her.

"Lana, it's him." He told her about the Wikipedia page he had just found. These parrots get yellow in old age. All on their face.

And so the two, Lana and her date, went back to staring at each other, overwhelmed by a coincidence that could not be.

When she told me this story, typing it in full late that night after their dinner on a kind of crazy excited high that only comes when you're sure you've met your soul mate and this amazing story must have brought you together, it took my breath away.

"THE SAME BIRD?!" I wrote back, screeching in caps lock. "But that's not possible," I continued.

And as I went to bed that night, I was certain these two would marry each other, the parrot walking them down the aisle.

"This will be the story we tell at your wedding, you realize?" I went on.

They didn't get married, of course, and the relationship soon began to fizzle. As Lana was weighing what to do— Why didn't she have stronger feelings? Maybe she should stick it out longer? Was this as good as it gets?—I wasn't the only one to think of the story.

Because in what world can a man find your discarded parrot on the street twenty years before and then not become your betrothed? It was too amazing, too strange, too fantastical, I thought. Twenty years. The same bird!

The answer, of course, is this: our world.

A world in which every day we can be blinded by stories of such sparkle and fun that we *should* wake each morning hoping and expecting such splendor. A world in which we aren't reduced to expecting less, but to expecting more. Expecting more whimsy and joy than we can ever imagine.

LOOK FOR HELP IN THE RIGHT PLACES

One day, I was looking at our credit card statements when I saw a charge from "Netflix Movies" that we had been getting for a couple of months. We'd never signed up for Netflix, although I'd always meant to, so I called the phone number printed next to the charge to see what was going on. It connected me to an audio recording of a diet commercial. After thirty seconds, the phone automatically disconnected. I did this five times, and the same thing happened, again and again.

Eventually, I realized this wasn't working and called the credit card company directly, who told me it was some scam they had seen before. "Netflix Movies" was not the Netflix you and I know. They quickly fixed the charges.

In the end, the number I had been calling erroneously was of course not a customer service number associated with a DVD rental organization, but rather the phone number of the scam operation. And it got me thinking about problems, and how we look for people to help us solve them, and how we often look in the wrong place or go to the wrong person.

Every time we have a problem we can't solve, the key to the solution is to figure out who in the world might truly be invested in helping you. Whether for financial motives, emotional reasons, or otherwise, that is the person who will truly provide you the help you need. It is your job to figure out who that is and how to enlist them.

If we have a faulty credit card charge from a scam company, that company has no interest in reversing it, obviously, or even picking up the phone. In contrast, the credit card company, which doesn't want to lose my business, does want to help. When we book a flight for the wrong day and need to call the airline to change it, the airline might have an interest in helping you—if you fly a lot, say, and they are worried about losing your business.

If you need to clean the windows in your house and you live alone, the only other person who might be invested in helping you solve the problem is likely someone you can pay to fix it. And a window cleaning company with less business, rather than more, might care more than the one that can't keep track of its orders. Maybe. (Or maybe not.)

When we have a problem and we need help, it's an act

of meditation and an act of balance. *Meditating* on who else cares about our problem and *balancing* out what it is that can motivate him or her to help us.

When we realize this, everything changes, and we see for the first time that our biggest job when faced with a problem is figuring out who the right person is to help us, and then thinking about a way to get them to do so. Practice makes perfect, and the practice in this exercise is asking, opening your hands and widening your smile and saying, "I need help," or "Can you lend a hand?", or "Can I hire you to do this thing for me?"

For those of us not used to asking, this can be the hardest moment. The moment you make a break with a past of doing it all and going it alone. But it can be the most important break you ever make, and one of the best things you ever do.

So go ahead, make the ask. Find the right person, and tell them you need the help you need to do the things you need to do.

READ MORE

A s a child, I *loved* to read.
In grade school, it was a relatively good thing. As I plowed through books like it was my job, my parents heard about how "advanced" of a reader I was. *She reads at an 8th grade level! She reads at a 10th grade level! She reads like a college student!*

In high school, the busiest time of my life until that point so far, reading took more of a back seat than I wanted. I slept little, did homework all the time, ran ragged at sports practices, and on the rare occasion that I had a free moment I spent it obsessing over college. But on vacations things were different. On vacations we'd go away for a week and I'd tear through ten books. *This is what I was meant to be doing, I'd sigh.* And then I'd be back in real life, where we read a mere ten pages a week in the cruddy English class at my cruddy high school.

In college, I had more free time than in high school

(something about not having to be in class for eight hours a day helped that), and reading for pleasure and personal knowledge came back into my life. A bit.

In the years after college, though, my world opened again, like it had when I was as a child. Suddenly, I had so many more hours in which I could read. Sure there was work, and family and friends and all the regular sorts of life commitments we sign up for by the sheer nature of becoming adults, but—more or less—I owned my time more than I did in the past.

And it was in this era that I realized that not everyone read like I did. Worse than that, I realized that most people thought it was weird the lengths to which I'd go to read anywhere and everywhere.

When I spent the year traveling around the world with Lara, she once did a hysterical photographic series of pictures of me reading in places where I should have clearly been absorbing the view. It was as if, in my adult years, I became incapable of going anywhere without a book.

Which is exactly what it was, in fact. These days, no matter where I go, I have a book in hand, and it baffles me the number of people I see who don't do the same. How many lines do I stand in where the vast majority of people around me are simply staring off into space? Decompressing is good, and taking a moment to zone out may be a positive thing, but can this really be our norm? All the time? For most people?

One early morning as I was passing through immigration in some port in the United States, this all came to a head.

It was five in the morning, or thereabouts, and the line was horrid. We'd been waiting easily for forty minutes at this point, and I'd been reading the whole time. Most of my fellow passengers were not doing the same, and those who weren't trying to soothe wriggling babies or talking with their traveling companions just stared off into space.

At one point, two men traveling together looked at me, momentarily stunned, and said: "You're reading? At five in the morning? How can you do that?"

I responded, just as baffled, "How can you not?"

We stared at one another awkwardly and then decided to part ways, the distance between our two perspectives too great to overcome. I'm a reader, you see. And that was the only way to explain it.

In reality, I think most people are readers at heart.

Tons of studies tell us why reading makes us smarter and more informed. Many thought leaders claim that reading is a key predictor of success in business and in life.

If you already love reading, you are lucky. Lucky in that challenging yourself to read more will simply include finding more time in your life to do so. If you don't already love reading, however, you need to start there.

Either way, start small.

If you want to find more time in your life for the reading you already love, add ten minutes of reading a day on your lunch break or when you wake in the morning or right before you get on the elliptical or when you're—yes—waiting in line at customs. Finding these moments and learning that these moments exist all around you will help you realize you have the power to create more.

If your challenge is finding a passion for reading (for the first time, or once again), start small there as well. Find a short book with a message that you can't wait to learn about. Don't go for meaty nonfiction, but rather something light, fun, and guaranteed to entice you. Short stories? A mystery? Find something that lights any spark of interest. Over time, you can build your reading muscle to start branching out into other genres.

Read more, so you can read more.

Your life will thank you.

LET GO

When I met Sammy in the orphanage where he lived, the first day I was there, the day that was not supposed to become a year, I didn't know where things would lead. But I knew that I was meeting someone important, and someone who might change my life.

The journey to bring Sammy to the United States, and then to shepherd him through the years since, has been harder than I ever imagined. Don't get me wrong: by all objective measures, his story is a good one. He has thrived. He has won awards. He has flown all over the world on behalf of organizations that want to hear his story. He has written a book. He has worked tirelessly on behalf of those who need a champion. He has used his one life well.

But he hasn't done everything I have wanted him to do. And therein lies the problem, you see. Because I have strong ideas about what people should do and what they shouldn't and why they should listen to me and why I know everything and why my way is the better way.

My parents once gave me a postcard that hangs on my refrigerator. It reads: The world is not yet perfect, and I'm getting impatient.

Sammy is someone who makes me very impatient. *I can't sit around and watch a teenager mess up*, I'll say to my husband. *I can't stand to watch him make the wrong decision*, I'll moan.

And then I'll write another strongly worded email. I LOVE YOU! I'll write at the end, in caps lock, as if that seals the deal.

Now he'll do what I tell him to do, I think.

And yet again, he won't.

And yet again, I'll moan.

And yet again, I'll complain to my parents and they'll say the same thing they've always said: this is parenting. Get used to letting them go.

And then my seven-month-old will reach for the pickle juice and I'll tell her she's not going to like it but she'll keep reaching anyway. And when she doesn't understand me (she's seven months old, after all), I'll sigh and say, "Well, she has to learn it herself. This will teach her."

And then she'll surprise us all by licking up the sour stuff like there's no tomorrow and reaching for more. Because she knew best, all along.

Because the world is not yet perfect and we all need to learn to let it go.

WRITE NOW

My father is a writer—a journalist, a book writer, a lover of words. A man who never wanted his daughter to do the same. While I was growing up, he always said he would like to cut off my hands so I wouldn't follow suit. He never did it, and this here book is (one) result.

Writing, for writers, is often more of a curse than a blessing. A need that must be filled. A longing that must be met. Something—simply—that must be done.

When I don't write, I yearn for it.

I idealize it in a way I cannot explain. I think of isolated cabins and remote lakes and me, a pen in hand, writing my way to the next great something.

This is not reality. Reality is forcing myself to sit down and type.

Reality is me booking an eleven-day solo cruise without my fiancé to write the first draft of a book. Reality is missing my business school graduation because I sit, two blocks away, completing my final edits before sending a manuscript to a publisher. Reality is scheduling a weekend at a hotel away from my husband and new, small baby in order to get words onto paper. Reality is going to an Internet-less café and drinking six decaf lattes in the span of one ten-hour day to edit a manuscript. But the harsh reality of writing (Cruise ships! Hotels! Lattes!) doesn't take away from the joy that writing—the writing once it's written, perhaps—does give me.

Because, writing, at its heart, gives me two great gifts.

First, it gives me the chance to create something. By typing away, I can create a thing that I know I made.

Second, it is expression at its finest. By putting pen to page I pour out the creative me.

Both are gifts for different sides of me.

Writing means different things to different people. For people who define themselves as writers, writing is often more about the creation. Non-writers, people who do not in some way define themselves this way, see different things from beginning a writing practice. It's more therapeutic, perhaps, more grounded in expression than in creation.

Both are essential. And I believe that both can do immensely positive things in your own life. Starting a writing practice—even a simple daily practice of three minutes of jotting down what you think on a legal pad—can have enormous benefits for your health and your state of mind. It can help you understand what you really feel, make decisions in times of trial, and better push for what you really want.

There is no better advice than to write, and write now.

TRACK YOUR DAYS

The concept of evaluating your days is not new. I've talked about doing it during my morning routine, and many productivity gurus tout its wisdom. It works because it makes sense.

If we don't have a goal, we'll never get where we want to go. And if we don't stop and evaluate where we are, we'll never know if we're there.

In the spirit of small life hacks that make a big difference, I can't stress enough the importance of looking back and asking:

What was the best thing I did today?

You might be intrigued, and surprised, by some of the answers. Yes, it might be the obvious: "When I ate chocolate ice cream," or "When I watched the game."

But it might also be something more unexpected. "*When I read for five minutes in the waiting room,*" or "*When I was running and it started raining,"* or *"When I played with my daughter when she woke up at three a.m."* Whatever it is, this question aims to help you figure out if you can do more of that thing in order to make every day better.

Now, I don't stop there, and I typically go further to ask another question:

What was the best thing I did last week?
And,
What was the best thing I did last month?

If you ask yourself these simple questions, you're bound to find out some unexpected and illuminating things about yourself and the ways you spend your time. Most important, you'll see some guideposts to how you should be better spending your time in the future. I'm a fan for doing this with great regularity, and what I find most amazing about this practice is that it isn't hard or scientific, but it is immediately rewarding. By simply looking at a week's worth of days tracked, I can see what it is that I like doing most, and what I should be doing more of. By expanding that—and looking at a whole month's worth—I learn even more. How am I really spending my days and how do I want to be spending them better?

Simple tracking can lead to simple changes.

BE ON YOUR HOLIDAY BEST, ALL YEAR ROUND

A t the holidays, we try to be our best. We dust off our fancy red tuxedos and pointy Santa hats, we clean off our makeup brushes and poof our hair to its heights. And for good reason. During the holidays, we see everyone we know. For those of us who go home to friends and family—or live in places where friends and family come to us—the holiday season is a time when *we are seen*. And so, we want to be at our best.

This doesn't just apply to us. I'm likely not the only one who has recommended a particular outfit for a sometimes-clueless husband or an always-clueless minor to wear to a particular event. (No matter if it's a Christmas Eve church service or an ugly sweater party.) We want us all to be our best, and we work hard to that aim.

Our holiday attire is just the tip of the iceberg. During the holidays we don't just dress better, but we try to bake better, smile better, make better party banter, and just *be better*, in general.

But it's a funny thing that we do all this, and work so hard, and spend so much time being our best, for only a few weeks a year. After all, wouldn't it be great to be this way all year long? To be on top of our game a whole fifty-two weeks a year?

In a word: yes.

This year, when you're full up with the excitement of December, sit and think about the three best things you present during this time. The three best things you exude to the world—be it your hospitality, your charm, your wit, your winning smile, your knack for logistical wrangling, or your baked goods—and dedicate yourself to trying to bring these into your life throughout the year, long after your New Year's resolutions lose their January luster.

After all, if we're at our best in the cold depths of December, it's not a far stretch to say that we can one day be at our best in the bright sun of June. (If you live in the Southern hemisphere, like I do, just go ahead and flip that last sentence on its head.)

BUILD ON SMALL, EARLY WINS

One day in the middle of last year, I had one of those days. No, not one of those days when you lie around in pajamas eating nachos and wondering why your big project isn't getting done, but the *other* kind.

The kind where you know you're on fire. The kind where you just keep churning and churning through your to-do list and even when the day should be over you put in a few extra hours because the fire just won't go out. And then, when you finally do close your laptop and turn off the phone, you wonder why a *New York Times* journalist isn't knocking down your door to ask, "So how did you do it? How did you become the MOST PRODUCTIVE PERSON ON THE PLANET IN ONE DAY?!?"

That day was amazing.

And then the next day, the whole nachos thing happened.

When I pulled myself out of bed with a belly full of cheese, I started wondering about what it is that made that one day so amazing, and then the next day such an overwhelming dud. How did I manage to be so productive, and what's the lesson on how to be productive in general? And—gasp—how could I get myself to do that *every* day?

I came up with a couple of thoughts.

By Definition, Insane Productivity Can't Happen Every Day of the Week

Sadly, insane productivity cannot happen every day. None of us can fire on all cylinders every day of the week. Or, when we do, we quickly experience burn out. As such, truly incredible productivity by definition has to happen infrequently. That way, your body and mind can rest and recuperate well to get ready to do it all again. That said, there are ways to maximize your life so that you do it on a more regular basis than you're doing now.

Productivity Builds on Productivity

The day I was so on fire didn't start out that amazing. But there was a moment at which I made a decision to put my head down. Just for a short period of dedicated hard work. And, as happens when you successfully get through a short period of good, solid work, you feel psychologically awesome and want more. That's what happened that day. Small wins built on small wins, and by the end of the day I was on such a streak that I wanted to keep going.

Ultimately, what I learned in thinking about why I had such a good day—and then why I had such a bad day—was that I simply can't have those amazing feats of productive genius every day. But I can have them sometimes. And to make them happen, I have to set myself up for success by building on small, early wins.

Try it, today.

DO LESS
TO DO MORE

Although I love everything related to productivity—from understanding how to really rock it, to making small tweaks that yield big results, to learning how my body can work alongside my mind—there is one area of productivity that is still a wasteland for many an aspiring productivity hack like me.

That area?

The productivity involved in doing less.

I'm not talking about the concept of "flow" here (when you're so much in the zone that you're rocking it out and feel great). Instead, I'm talking about a strange, less understood type of productivity that happens when you think you're not making progress, but you actually are.

A woman I know teaches massage, and she always tells me that the key to moving our bodies well and to enjoying all that our bodies are made for is to learn to do less. Every day, when you sit on a chair, or squat on the floor, or stand up tall, you should ask yourself: How Can I Do Less? Because our bodies know the way, but our mind often confuses things.

One year, I spent nine months of my life enjoying the productivity of doing less. That year, I was pregnant.

When you're pregnant, there's this magical thing happening inside you (a life is being created! a tiny lentil-sized human is taking shape!) and yet you're not really doing all that much to make it happen. You throw up, you take naps, you hang out with doctors. But your efforts are really quite minimal in comparison to all that's really going on behind the scenes.

And in terms of your regular life, all bets are off. Some women plow forward and live and work as they do in a normal year. In my case, I was doing way, *way* less than normal. And yet, despite the fact that my professional projects were at a complete standstill and I was basically lying in bed watching *House Hunters International* all day, I was actually, amazingly, "being productive." In fact, I think most people could argue I was the most productive I've ever been. (Making a human trumps writing a book or having a successful career, right?)

Overwhelmingly, this taught me that we ultimately

don't always know when we're truly being productive, and when we're just spinning our wheels. Sure, sometimes we might have superhuman productive days or weeks where we know we produced, but other times we might have little indication that huge strides are actually being made behind the scenes.

So what's the lesson here?

Look behind the curtain to see what's really happening. Is there true productive growth going on? Is a critical framework being laid? In all your efforts, take more time to try to see where you are "really" being productive, and not just where you *think* you are.

And always seek the Holy Grail: the place where you can do less, to do more.

DISCONNECT

Don't get me wrong, I love my connected life. I love an Apple TV that allows me to tune into anything I want, a Jawbone that tracks my sleep and steps, and an iPhone that makes it easy to Facetime with family half a globe away.

But even I (or especially I, perhaps) know the importance of taking breaks. Whether small or big, breaks are good for every digital soul. But taking a digital break in this day and age isn't something you can do all at once. You can't just pull the plug, so to speak.

What you can do is put some good preparation into it, and then reap the benefits. When I take a digital break—of two days, or two weeks—here's how I plan ahead to stay sane without my technology:

Prepare Beforehand

I didn't wake up yesterday and decide to go offline today. Instead, I planned ahead of time. Since I'm a blogger, have a social media presence, and have a work life that keeps me connected, I need to prepare ahead of time to go off the grid. So I schedule blog posts to go out, and program certain social media updates. I set auto-responders on my email addresses alerting folks to my vacation, and tell them what to do in my absence. I get ready, Freddy, and you should, too.

Allow Yourself a Little Bit

A total technological blackout is sometimes a good thing. One year, I took a twelve-day complete digital break and loved almost every minute of it. It felt like a true digital detox, in every sense of the word. The first couple of mornings I could practically feel the shakes as I instinctively reached for my iPhone, ready to scroll through my emails and tweets before getting out of bed. My only "cheat" was to receive text messages if something crazy happened and I had to get online. In about twelve days, I received ten messages, one of which was actually important. (It was about the pope, and it got me online in a flash.)

Some years, and most every Saturday, I don't do such a total blackout. Instead, I'll stay off my computer, but check emails occasionally on my iPhone. Since

I hate typing on my iPhone as is, this will keep me out of the email fray, which makes up the bulk of my blood-pressure inducing digital non-delights.

Always Have a Back-up Plan

In the case of most of my digital breaks, by allowing myself some time on my iPhone to scan for emergent fires, I don't usually need to open my computer. That said, I'm always ready to do so if need be. In my more extreme digital blackouts, when email on my phone is also off-limits, I allow for urgent text messages to call me back into the fray. Your system might be similar, or it might be different, but either way, the key is this: have a back-up plan, trust in that plan, and then let yourself truly disconnect.

In our connected world, I believe that digital breaks aren't a luxury, but a necessity. Something we all need to do to reset our lives to what is truly important, and to remember what we really need to care about as we move forward. Indeed, digital breaks make it possible for us to keep overwhelm at bay.

BELIEVE IN
THE POWER OF
SMALL THINGS TO
CHANGE YOUR LIFE

A funny thing happened on the fourth of April. I woke up, pregnant, and had a good day. Some work, some play, some rest. In close to a month I'd be having a baby, and I was settling into that stretch of pregnancy where you are uncomfortably large and eager for it all to be behind you.

At night, I went to bed.

A few hours later, I woke up to find that my water had broken. Since I didn't really know what that meant, I had to Google to understand if that was really what was going on. But Google wasn't very definitive about the whole thing, so I called Lara, now a doctor. She hemmed and hawed. Maybe it's broken. Maybe it's not. And so then I called the midwife. I still hadn't met her, and I'd been meaning to go to a few of her classes in the month to come. She said more of the same. Maybe, maybe not.

Then I called my parents. It was the middle of the night in California also, and I talked on the answering machine for a while until someone picked up the phone. It was my father, disoriented, and when I told him I thought I was in labor he said, half asleep—"That's nice honey. Good luck with that,"—and tried to hang up the phone. I told him to wake up my mother.

By the time I finished talking to her, I was pretty sure that things were moving along. A pain started that felt like a tiny little cramp. A bit later, I noticed the cramp again, ever so slightly. By the third time I thought, *could this be a contraction?*

We started timing it, just to be safe. Seven minutes apart, then six.

Throughout it all, I kept saying the same thing to my husband, "Do you think I'm really in labor?" And then, as it became clearer, "I can't believe I really might be in labor."

And then I remembered that they had told me to eat.

All my friends who'd gone through labor had said the same thing: "Eat before you go to the hospital!" I had a plan in my head. I would go to a drive-thru (fast food! indulgence!) on the way to the hospital. But I was hungry now, so I knew I could no longer wait for the drive-thru. I went down to the kitchen and made myself a huge chicken quesadilla. I poured on lots of salsa.

"Are you sure you don't want something more bland?" my husband asked, ever so quietly, not wanting to upset the ravenous one.

I made mincemeat of his question.

"No!" I boomed.

(And later, when the midwife asked who on earth fed me so much, I tried to make it look like it wasn't my idea.)

The contractions kept coming, and the midwife told us to come into the hospital.

We packed a bag and started driving.

A lot of things happened over the next few hours. The car broke down, we had to take a taxi to the hospital, and the labor was harder than I ever imagined it would be. And then it was done.

And at the end of it all, there was a sweet babe. A sweet girl I'd longed for years for. A tiny thing a bit too eager to see the world.

The whole time, I was a broken record, saying the same thing to José and to anyone else who would listen, "I can't believe this is really happening."

And I wasn't just saying it; I actually, truly, could not really believe that it was happening, because it was different than I had imagined, and what I had imagined was never really fully formed in my mind anyway.

Back when my friends and I graduated from college, it was a huge moment. We were twenty-two, and not much else had happened in most of our lives, and this was one of the biggest changes we would ever go through. College had turned us from kids to adults, and now we were being set loose on the world. To top it all off, we were all moving to different spots on the globe, and everyone was nervous and scared about it all.

But the morning we left, and we danced in front of the airport vans as each person rode off to the airport, we didn't find ourselves on the pavement, crying our final tears. And because of this, my friend Amalia and I came up with the theory that sometimes when the big things happen in life you can't actually process them at the time they happen. Sometimes, you can only really understand them in retrospect. Because sometimes they are too big for the small moments.

When Lucia was born, it was just like that. She was a tiny little thing who was too big for my life. Too big for me to yet believe in, and just small enough to change my life.

DO THE THING THAT YOU CAN DO

My grandmother, Ma, can't go to church anymore. She's doing pretty well, don't get me wrong. She's ninety-two, and still lives alone, and still drives short distances to get her groceries, and is sharp as a tack. But walking long distances is harder, and the church hasn't figured out their parking very well, and the weather is often a mess where she lives, and the eighty-six-year-old man, who was secretly in love with her and who always waited for her in the pew they shared, died last year.

So church is out.

But she's okay with this. She went to church her whole life, and she understands that church, like her bridge group or her shoulder mobility, wasn't meant to last forever. But what she learned at church *was*. At least that's the way she says it.

Instead of going to church, Ma bakes cakes.

Not a lot and not too often. After all, it doesn't make much sense to make a big old cake when you live alone. But sometimes she does.

One day last fall she got out all the ingredients. It took a while, of course. She pulled out the stool to reach the top shelf in her spotless kitchen. And then, again and again, she got up on the stool, held on to the cupboard with one hand, and with the other pulled down what she needed to make the apple cake. And when it was done, after she'd put the final touches of powdered sugar all over the top, she sighed.

And then she began cutting. Because, of course, there's no way she could eat the whole cake. It would be hard for her to eat an entire piece, if we're being honest. So first she cut a big hunk and gave it to the Russian woman next door. And then she gave another hunk to the caretaker of the man who lives below her. And then she called up her other downstairs neighbor, the squirrely one, the ex-teacher who is in her seventies but sometimes looks decades older.

And Ma said to her over the phone, "I'd like to bring you some cake." But this neighbor wasn't so sure.

"Well, what's in it?" she asked, skeptically.

And Ma explained. It has apple and flour and lots of sugar and some vanilla and some cinnamon and some nutmeg and some powdered sugar, and the list went on. The neighbor agreed, begrudgingly, and so Ma wrapped up the piece of cake and carried it down to her.

And then Ma came home, closed the door, and sat down to eat her own piece. She'd spent all day baking, had given away all but this one piece, and was now ready to enjoy it.

And then the phone rang again. It was the neighbor, that squirrely one, the one who never seems to have enough visitors and always seems to be anxious about something. The one who wasn't so sure about that cake.

"Can you bring me more of that cake?" she asked abruptly. No greeting. No thanks.

Ma looked at her last piece, the piece she hadn't yet cut into, and she shook her head. And she took it downstairs. Because she can't go to church, she says, but she can do this.

As for me, I cannot cook. I cannot play football. I cannot wash a window well, or parallel park on a hill, or give you directions to most anyplace, anywhere. There is a whole long list of things I cannot do.

But there are things I can do. A lot of them. And you've got a whole list of your own.

No matter where you are in life, do the small thing that

you can do, today. The thing that will help you and will help someone else right where you both are.

This is a great way to change a world.

CONCLUSION

We all want a better life. But sometimes, getting there doesn't feel so easy, or so fun.

When you lace up your running shoes to pound the pavement, say. Or when you have a difficult conversation you've been putting off. When you get up early to teach Sunday school even though what you really feel like doing is sleeping in.

For me, and for many, it's my faith in God that pushes me over the edge in these times. Faith that reminds me why I'm doing what I'm doing and what I'm doing it all for. Faith that makes it worth the while.

Turning a life on its head is hard work, and most of us have too much going on anyway to make massive, radical changes from one day to the next. Nor does that kind of change usually work to make a lasting difference in our lives.

Instead, I believe the key to big change (and a big, better life) is small change. Small steps, one after another, that lead to bold changes and bright new lives. In this book, we've looked at a number of small ways that, over time, will lead to big results. Do one thing. Then try another. Along the way, have a reason for it all. Over time you can see yourself being built into the new better you that you've always wanted to be.

I'll be cheering you on, as I do the same.

Here's to *The Better Life*, right where you are.

RESOURCES

Here is a short list of some of my favorite books on living better:

- *Rework*, Jason Fried and David Heinemeier Hansson
- *What the Most Successful People Do Before Breakfast*, Laura Vanderkam
- *The Power of Full Engagement*, Jim Loehr and Tony Schwartz
- *The Power of Habit*, Charles Duhigg
- *Flow: The Psychology of Optimal Experience*, Mihaly Csikszentmihalyi
- *The Willpower Instinct*, Kelly McGonigal
- *The Way We're Working Isn't Working*, Tony Schwartz
- *The Clockwork Muse*, Eviatar Zerubavel
- *Bird by Bird*, Anne Lamott
- *Accidental Genius, Using Writing to Generate Your Best Ideas, Insight, and Content*, Mark Levy

THE BETTER LIFE

- *Start: Punch Fear in the Face, Escape Average, and Do Work That Matters*, Jon Acuff
- *Vision Map: Charting a Step-by-Step Course for Your Biggest Hopes and Dreams*, Joël Malm
- *The Well-Balanced World Changer*, Sarah Cunningham
- *Slowing Down to the Speed of Life*, Richard Carlson and Joseph Bailey
- *The Happiness Project*, Gretchen Rubin
- *Beyond the Sky and the Earth,* Jamie Zeppa
- *Internal Time*, Till Roenneberg

ACKNOWLEDGMENTS

B ooks are fun, but not when you do them alone. Thankfully, I didn't.

Thanks to Randall Payleitner and the whole Moody team for vision and brawn.

Thanks to Esther Fedorkevich, Whitney Gossett and the Fedd Agency, for wisdom, laughs, and putrefied pies.

Thanks to my many friends and family members who inspired these stories. You are kind to appear in print, even when (barely) disguised.

Thanks to Jose and Lucia, and the Pennisetum.

ABOUT
THE AUTHOR

Claire Diaz-Ortiz is an author, speaker, and technology innovator who has been named one of the 100 Most Creative People in Business by Fast Company. Claire was an early employee at Twitter, Inc., where she spent five and a half years leading social innovation.

In Claire's time at Twitter, she was called everything from "The Woman Who Got the Pope on Twitter" (Wired) and "Twitter's Pontiff Recruitment Chief" (The Washington Post) to a "Force for Good" (Forbes) and "One of the Most Generous People in Social Media" (Fast Company).

Claire is the author of several books, including *Twitter for Good: Change the World One Tweet at a Time*; *Greater Expectations: Succeed (and Stay Sane) in an On-Demand, All-Access, Always-On Age*; and *Hope Runs: An American Tourist, a Kenyan Boy, a Journey of Redemption.*

She is a frequent international speaker on social media, business, and innovation and has been invited to deliver keynotes and trainings at organizations like the Vatican, the US State Department, Verizon, South by Southwest, TEDX, and many others.

She writes a popular business blog at ClaireDiazOrtiz .com and serves as a LinkedIn Influencer, one of a select group of several hundred global leaders chosen to provide original content on the LinkedIn platform.

Claire holds an MBA from Oxford University, where she was a Skoll Foundation Scholar for Social Entrepreneurship, and has a BA and an MA in anthropology from Stanford University.

She is the cofounder of Hope Runs, a nonprofit organization operating in AIDS orphanages in Kenya.

She has appeared widely in major television and print news sources such as CNN, BBC, *Time*, *Newsweek*, *The New York Times*, Good Morning America, The Today Show, *The Washington Post*, *Fortune*, *Forbes*, *Fast Company*, and many others.

Read more about her at
www.ClaireDiazOrtiz.com or via @claire on Twitter.

m moody collective

Join our email newsletter list to get resources and encouragement as you build a deeper faith.

Moody Collective brings words of life to a generation seeking deeper faith. We are a part of Moody Publishers, representing this next generation of followers of Christ through books on creativity, travel, the gospel, storytelling, decision making, leadership, and more.

We seek to know, love, and serve the millennial generation with grace and humility. Each of our books is intended to challenge and encourage our readers as they pursue God.

When you sign up for our newsletter, you'll get our emails twice a month. These will include the best of the resources we've seen online, book deals and giveaways, plus behind-the-scenes and extra content from our books and authors. Sign up at *www.moodycollective.com*.

a part of Moody Publishers

Other Moody Collective Books

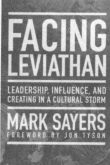

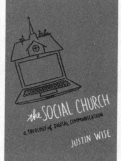